MOBILE NOTARY

SIDE HUSTLE OR BUSINESS

I0559037

THE GUIDE

$11,000 A MONTH MOBILE NOTARY

MARRIAGE OFFICIANT FINGERPRINT ROLLER

THINK OUTSIDE THE BOX

ATTORNEYS

CONVALESCENT HOSPITALS

LOAN SIGNING AGENT

CAR DEALERSHIPS

MORTGAGE COMPANIES

FIREARMS PERMIT

TITLE COMPANIES

BAIL BONDS COMPANIES

DELRAE HEMPHILL

Copyright © 2025 by **Delrae Hemphill**

All rights reserved. No part of this publication may be reproduced, distributed, or transmitted in any form or by any means, including photocopying, recording, or other electronic or mechanical methods, without the prior written permission of the copyright owner and the publisher, except in the case of brief quotations embodied in critical reviews and certain other noncommercial uses permitted by copyright law. For permission requests, write to the publisher, "Attention: Permissions Coordinator," to the address below.

Studio of Books LLC
5900 Balcones Drive Suite 100
Austin, Texas 78731
www.studioofbooks.org
Hotline: (254) 800-1183

Ordering Information:
Special discounts are available on quantity purchases by corporations, associations, and others. For details, contact the publisher at the address above.

Printed in the United States of America.

ISBN-13: Softcover: 978-1-968491-60-4
                eBook: 978-1-968491-61-1

Library of Congress Control Number: 2025917178

Table *of* Contents

FOREWORD

My journey as a notary started way back around 2008. The pay for a typical loan signing ranges between, $175.00 to $250.00 dollars. Notaries in my network knew there value and only accepted loan signings assignments that would pay our fees. Today, things are not the same and for that reason I've added a few more weapons to the arsenal which will allow you as a new or veteran notary to have $11,000.00 months no matter the season.

Mobile Notary Side Hustle or Business will cover some new and exciting ways to change your notary license into a money-making machine.

If you hold a notary commission, you're already in possession of one of the most overlooked licenses with the power to generate multiple streams of income. What often starts as a side hustle, with strategy and intention, evolve into a six-figure business. This book, "Mobile Notary Side Hustle or Business," is your roadmap to discovering, launching, and scaling a highly profitable notary-based business.

Most people think of notaries as people who simply stamp and sign documents. That surface level view misses the incredible potential and versatility within the field. Whether you're a newly commissioned notary, a mobile notary with years of experience, or someone who's looking to pivot into a new entrepreneurial path, this book will walk you through not just one, but eight dynamic ways to leverage your commission into BIG BUCKS!

Throughout this journey, you'll learn how to transition from a one-dimensional notary service to a multi-dimensional entrepreneur offering in-demand, specialized services. From becoming a sought-after Loan Signing Agent to offering Apostille services that allow documents to be used internationally, and my new favorite, working with bail bond companies. Each chapter is packed with actionable insights, real life case studies, pricing strategies, and business tips.

One of the key advantages of the notary business is mobility, both literal and figurative. Mobile notary services have boomed in this new economy, allowing professionals like you to control your hours, set your rates, and choose your clients. Add to that the explosive growth of Remote Online Notarization (RON), and you'll see how notaries can now serve clients from across the country and the globe right from the comfort of their home.

But this book doesn't stop at what services to offer. It also dives into how to run your notary business like a well-oiled machine. You'll learn how to craft an irresistible brand, develop a simple but effective marketing plan, and when the time is right, scale your operation by training others and earning passive income.

The notary field is evolving rapidly. With changing laws, increasing demand, and emerging digital platforms, the timing couldn't be better to build your empire. If you're ready to move beyond just stamping papers and start making real money, you're in the right place.

Notarypreneur. Remember this new word. An entrepreneur who turns a notary commission into a goldmine of opportunity.

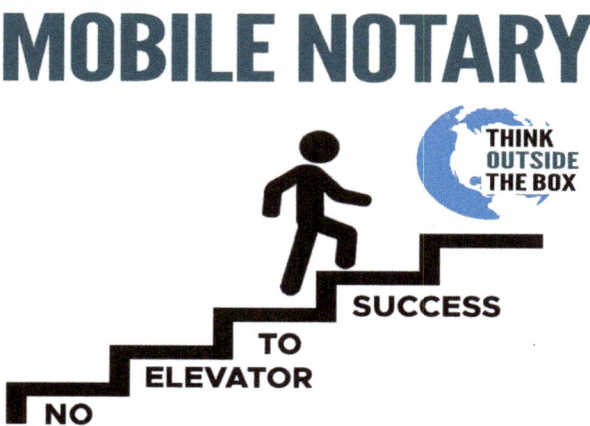

ACKNOWLEDGEMENTS

As a child, I dreamed of being famous and rich. My mother always told me that Big Dreamers make billionaires. Your unconditional love has made me feel like a Billionaire all my life. Thanks, Mom.

To my friends, Joi, Lenny, Gwenn, Hop, Terry, Tony, Kimaya, Ken, Roland, and Anne Marie. Thank you. You are the best.

To my daughter, SJ: Thank you for teaching me the true meaning of unconditional love. I love you more every second.

Special thanks to Jack Canfield, Oprah Winfrey, Tony Robbins, Nelson Mandela, Mel Robbin, Bishop Kenneth Ulmer, and Tom Brady. I read your books. I listen to your podcast and seminars. I study what you teach. How could I not be motivated to be a better version of myself? Thank you for sharing your knowledge and wisdom.

To my dad here on earth: I miss you. Dr. McBride, you may not have been my birth dad, but you were alright with me. I owe you a lot. Hope to see you again one day.

To the State of Hawaii. What an amazing place to be a student athlete on a football scholarship. The Aloha, the beauty, the peace and the friendly people. I can't thank you enough. What wonderful memories. Go Bows.

National Notary Association: You are an A LIST organization. Thank you for the incredible support, resources, and outstanding service you provide to notaries all around the world. The wealth of information from your staff and website is an invaluable resource for both new and experienced notaries alike.

INTRODUCTION

Congratulations! You have passed your State Notary Public Examination. All of your studying and sacrifice have paid off.

This Book was written to help you hit the ground running. It is designed as an aid to understanding the functionality of being a notary and all the wonderful possibilities. Truthfully, I wrote this book to help you 10X your notary license. Here is a breakdown of the potential income sources covered in this book right in the introduction. Let's Go!

Service potential	Monthly Income
Loan Signing Agent	$2,000 - $10,000
Bail Bonds Companies	$1,000 - $11,000
Mobile Notary	$1,500 - $7,500
Live Scan Fingerprinting	$1,000 - $6,000
Jail Signing Services	$2,000 - $10,000
"RON" Online Notary	$2,000 - $8,000
Power of Attorney	$500 - $4,000
Weddings (authorized states)	$1,000 - $9,000
Field Inspections	$500 - $2,500
Notary Permit Running	$300 - $2,200

Being a notary is one of the only professions or side hustles that I know of where you can turn a profit in the first month after receiving your notary commission.

CHAPTER 1

The Power of Your Notary Commission

Key Notes:

The Four F's

Finance, Freedom, Flexibility, Family

Your notary commission is far more than a rubber stamp. It's a golden skeleton key to a dozen unlocked doors leading to financial elevation. At first glance, getting that commission may have seemed like an extra credential, maybe a nice favor to friends and family. But the truth is hiding in plain sight? That little certificate of authority is a government-sanctioned superpower. It grants you legal gravitas to witness moments that shape lives. From signing off on real estate deals, confirming powers of attorney, witnessing the signing of wills, affirming wedding vows, sealing business partnerships across continents, and yes, even helping someone post bail. That last one, by the way, is one of the most underrated yet lucrative notary paths I've traveled to 10X my revenue.

Where trust is demanded, notaries rise. And in trust… lives opportunity.

The Unseen Currency of the Notary Seal

Your commission carries unspoken clout in a world starving for legitimate verification. With identity theft and forgery turning into modern-day plagues, businesses, legal systems, and global institutions are leaning heavily on notaries as gatekeepers of integrity.

Here's why this demand is surging:

- Remote work has created a vacuum for mobile and online notarization.
- Real estate chaos, driven by fluctuating interest rates, keeps loan signing agents constantly in rotation.
- Global commerce demands Apostille services to translate legality across borders.
- The silver tsunami, our aging population, requires notarized POAs and medical directives.
- Correctional systems rely on notaries to service incarcerated individuals behind walls.
- The digital age has birthed Remote Online Notarization (RON), letting you serve clients miles or even oceans away.

And the kicker? Depending on your state, your entry ticket costs barely $50 to $200. But if you wield it correctly, that tiny investment can metamorphose into a six-figure income.

The Notarypreneur's Treasure Map

So now what? You've got the seal. Here's how you weaponize it:

- Launch a local mobile notary outfit.
- Collaborate with realtors and title companies as a certified loan signing agent.
- Forge alliances with bail bond professionals and offer jail signing services.
- Handle Apostille authentication for those with international affairs.
- Set up a Remote online notary (RON) based operation and serve clients from your kitchen table.
- Assist families with end-of-life and estate planning documents.
- Work with hospitals, hospices, eldercare homes, and legal offices.
- Build a notary brand, sell templates, online guides, courses, and yes, even write books like this one.

You're not limited to one niche. Stack them. Blend them. Scale them. There are no rules except one: think like a CEO, not an ERRAND RUNNER.

Elevate Your Identity: Who You Truly Are

When you shift your perspective, you realize you're not just a notary, which I will repeat throughout this book. You're:

- A legal liaison
- A transactional technician
- A professional fixer
- A community cornerstone

And with that identity comes responsibility:

- Document everything like the IRS is your roommate.
- Always be marketing, even when you're not on the clock.
- Charge based on value delivered, not minutes burned.
- Use apps, CRM tools, automation or whatever it takes to work smart, not just hard.
- Show up like a pro: polished, punctual, and discreet.
- Study your state's notary laws like your license depends on it because it does.
- Get listed on directories like 123Notary, Notary Rotary, and Snapdocs.
- Solicit reviews like your business breathes on word of mouth.
- Secure your operation: bonding, E&O insurance, a business bank account, website, business cards.
- Arm yourself with tools: mobile printer, scanner, GPS, reliable wheels, and a secure briefcase.

Core Skills: Master the Basics Before You Fly

Before chasing big checks, master these fundamental tasks. They're your daily bread:

1. **Acknowledgments:** You're confirming the signer's identity and intent.
2. **Jurats:** The signer is swearing to the truth under oath.
3. **Oaths & Affirmations:** You're witnessing a verbal commitment of truth.
4. **Copy Certifications:** Ensuring a copy is an accurate twin of the original.
5. **Signature Witnessing:** Observing someone sign and verifying who they are.

These may seem like small potatoes. But stack urgency fees, travel rates, volume, and suddenly you're looking at serious cheddar. Think outside the box: hospitals, attorney firms, assisted living centers, jails, bail bonds, car dealers, real estate firms, and anyone in need of a professional certification or license. Opportunities are hiding in plain sight.

Numbers Don't Lie

Here's the math:

A notary doing general signings might bring in $200 to $400 per week, which is not bad for a side hustle. But one who gets certified as a Loan Signing Agent or works with bail bond companies? They could rake in $150 to $250 per appointment, often hitting three to five in a day, plus one late-night jail call if you're single like me and don't have to be home for dinner. That adds up to over $2,250 per week. Part-time hustle. Full-time results.

This journey? It kicks off in your mind. But momentum is what drives it forward. So keep pushing. Keep evolving. Keep stacking skills like bricks, and soon you'll have built an empire with nothing more than a seal, a signature, and a mindset unwilling to settle.

The next level is calling. Are You Ready?

CHAPTER 2

Becoming a Loan Signing Agent

Key Notes:

The Four F's

Finance, Freedom, Flexibility, Family

If you talk to successful notaries earning six figures or more annually, you'll find one common thread: **Loan Signings.**

The year was 2001. I was a successful Realtor with a great client base. Deals were consistent; however, little did I know that in 2009, my notary commission would become more important than my real estate license. What started off as a part-time hustle became my full-time source of income. My prior relationships with bank asset managers, escrow, and title companies saved me from having to seek employment in corporate America.

This chapter is your complete guide to understanding, entering, and thriving in the world of loan signings, a high-demand, high-reward field where your notary commission becomes a powerful income-generating tool.

Mark at Loan Signing System is a powerful resource.

A Loan Signing Agent is a notary public who specializes in notarizing documents related to real estate transactions.

These may include:

- Mortgage refinance packages
- Home equity line of credit (HELOC) docs
- Purchase and seller packages
- Reverse mortgage packages
- Loan modifications

You, as the loan signing agent, will walk the borrower through the loan documents to ensure everything is signed and notarized correctly. Once the loan documents have been signed and notarized, you will return the documents to the title or escrow company. Loan documents can either be mailed or sent electronically. It is very important to understand that it's not your job to explain the loan documents, only to **guide the signer through the process** and ensure every signature, initial, and notarization is done properly. Mistakes can delay funding or even cause a loan to fall through, which is why skilled LSAs are in high demand.

Nugget: I always bring an additional copy of the loan documents to each appointment.

Loan signings can earn $150 to $250 per signing and sometimes more for complex packages or same-day service. Let me repeat a simple formula for you.

Consider this:

- 3 signings a day × $150 per signing = $450/day
- 5 days a week = $2,250/week
- 4 weeks = **$9,000/month**

And many LSAs work part-time hours. That's the beauty of this niche: High earnings, flexible schedule, and enormous scalability.

Here's a checklist of essentials to become a professional Loan Signing Agent:

1. **Notary Commission**: The foundation. You must already be a commissioned notary in your state.

2. **Loan Signing Training & Certification**: Companies like the National Notary Association (NNA) and Loan Signing System (LSS) offer trusted courses that teach the documents, procedures, and how to pass background checks. If you are a Realtor, you should already be familiar with loan documents.

3. **Background Check**: Required by most signing services and title companies to ensure you're trustworthy.

4. **E&O Insurance (Errors & Omissions)**: Protects you against financial loss if you make a mistake on a document. Minimum $25,000 to $100,000 coverage is recommended. I personally started with $100,000 of E&O Insurance.

5. **Laser Printer (Dual Tray):** You'll need to print large packages of 100 to 150 pages in both letter and legal size paper.

6. **Scanner (High Speed):** Many title companies require scan backs before the package is mailed out. For the first six years, I never needed a scanner.

7. **Mobile Phone and Reliable Transportation:** You'll often need to travel to the signer's home, office, or even coffee shops.

Certification courses are great for building knowledge, but confidence comes from **doing**. To build confidence:

- Practice printing and organizing loan docs
- Review sample packages available in most LSA training
- Role play with friends or family
- Read every document and understand its purpose
- Learn how to respond to common signer questions with neutral, professional language

For example:

Signer: What's this 'Right to Cancel' document?

You: This document gives you three business days to cancel this refinance if you choose. It explains your rights under federal law.

This is extremely important. For this reason alone, I always bring an extra copy of the loan docs. You're not advising they're responsible for understanding their loan; you're simply guiding.

To earn consistently, you need a solid source of assignments. Here are the top channels: Please check for changes of address or phone numbers.

> **Signing Services**: These are companies that connect LSAs with title companies. They take a cut but offer steady work. California Companies:

Wendy Lewis Mobile Notary & Loan Signing Agent: Hayward, CA

- Website: wendylewisnotary.com
- Address: 27526 Tampa Ave Ste B, Hayward, CA 94544
- Phone: (510) 517-2494

Betancourt Notary Public and Loan Signing Services: Fresno, CA

- Website: liliett-the-notary.yolasite.com
- Address: 5627 N Figarden Dr Ste 116, Fresno, CA 93722
- Phone: (559) 840-9009

David's Mobile Notary Public & Loan Signing Agent: Fresno, CA

- Website: Google Maps
- Address: Fresno, CA 93711
- Phone: (559) 287-8496

Rapid Mobile Notary & Loan Signing Services: Sacramento, CA

- Website: rapidcsi.com
- Address: 4737 Rustic Rd, Fair Oaks, CA 95628
- Phone: (916) 500-4673

Loans & Notary: Lathrop, CA

- Website: satinderjitsingh.com
- Address: 17209 Bach Ct, Lathrop, CA 95330
- Phone: (408) 859-9682

Sandip Notary and Loan Signing Services: Pleasanton, CA

- Website: sandipnotary.com
- Address: 586 Touriga Ct, Pleasanton, CA 94566
- Phone: (815) 762-1385

Elite Signature Services: Chatsworth, CA

- Website: elitesignatureservices.com
- Address: 21000 Devonshire St, Chatsworth, CA 91311
- Phone: (818) 835-0825
- RLF Closing Services, LLC

Direct Work:

1. **Title & Escrow Companies:** This is where the real money is. By building relationships with local title companies, you can cut out the middleman and earn the full fee. Often $150 to $200 per appointment.

2. **Real Estate Agents & Mortgage Brokers:** Network with these professionals. They can refer clients and even help you get noticed

by title companies.

3. **Notary Directories & Platforms**: List yourself on platforms like 123notary, Notary Rotary, and one of my favorites, NNA. Make sure to attend the NNA yearly conference to increase visibility and meet notaries from other states.

Let's say you're based in a suburban city. Here's a typical day:

- 9:00 AM - Print and prepare docs for a 10 AM signing
- 10:00 AM - Complete signing at client's home (45 minutes)
- 11:00 AM - Drop off docs at FedEx, scan and email confirmation to escrow
- 11:30 PM - Lunch break and print docs for a 1 PM signing
- 1:00 PM - Seller signing at a real estate office
- 2:30 PM - Final signing of the day, a HELOC at a local Starbucks
- 3:45 PM - Scan, upload docs, and confirm delivery
- Done by 4:30 PM with $400 earned

All in one day. And that's just the beginning. Becoming a Loan Signing Agent is one of the most profitable decisions you can make with your notary commission.

The combination of flexibility, high pay, and constant demand creates a perfect storm of opportunity.

But remember that this is a business. Treat it like one. Invest in your education, your presentation, and your relationships. The more you sharpen your skills and expand your network, the more consistent and lucrative your bookings will be.

Side Bar: A wise man once said, "If you can find something to do in your life that financially supports you, gives you the freedom and flexibility to spend quality time with family and friends, then you are on the right track to finding either your passion or your purpose."

CHAPTER 3

Apostille Services Going Global

Key Notes:

The Four F's

Finance, Freedom, Flexibility, Family

Welcome to the enigmatic yet fertile realm of apostille services. An overlooked goldmine for savvy notaries willing to unshackle themselves from zip code thinking and step into the global paper chase. I reside in California, and let me tell you, the hunger for apostille assistance right now is ravenous.

In this chapter, we'll crack open the what, why, and how behind apostilles and, more importantly, how you can morph this cross-border necessity into a consistent, high-paying stream of revenue that doesn't sleep.

What on Earth is an Apostille?

An apostille is not a wizard's stamp, though it may as well be. It's a sovereign-level authentication bestowed by a certified authority in a nation belonging to the Hague Apostille Convention of 1961. Its job? To verify the integrity of public documents so they hold water overseas.

Put plainly, if someone in the U.S. needs to send official papers like a marriage license, diploma, or a durable power of attorney to another country, those papers must not only be notarized but also apostilled; otherwise, they're just fancy paper.

As a notary, you're the gatekeeper. No, you don't craft the apostille yourself, but you become the architect of the process. Your mission:

- Decode the bureaucratic mumbo jumbo for your client.
- Submit everything to the correct agency (usually the Secretary of State).
- Orchestrate the whole logistical ballet from signature to international shipment.

Why the Stampede for Apostille Services?

There's a tidal wave of students, digital nomads, expats, and global entrepreneurs who need their documents internationally legit. I recently

Google expat services in Panama and Mexico for personal travel, and more than 20 verified apostille-related listings popped up with full contact information. Translation? That's the sound of a cash register going ***cha-ching.***

Here's the human side of it:

- A student from Guadalajara needs their U.S. transcripts certified.
- An American couple wants to tie the knot in Tuscany, birth certificates please.
- A nonprofit coordinating overseas adoptions needs an apostilled intent letter.
- A startup branching into South America must legalize its incorporation documents.
- A single mom jetting with her toddler needs their birth certificates apostilled.

These aren't just documents, they're high-stakes, time-sensitive lifelines. And people will fork over serious cash for someone who doesn't botch the job.

What Should You Charge?

This isn't $10 per-signature territory anymore. Apostille services are usually billed at a premium flat rate, above and beyond your notary fees. You can confidently charge between $100 and $250 per document, depending on:

- Speed same-day or overnight delivery.
- Number and type of documents.
- Door-to-door service.
- Degree of bureaucratic nightmare involved.
- Extras like translation or shipping.

Some notaries elevate the experience and package it as an apostille concierge service. Handling notarization, prepping, legwork, and international delivery as a bundle. That kind of white glove treatment can command $300 to $500 plus per client, easily.

Who's Your Ideal Audience?

Once you're fully operational, these are your primary cash cows:

- Immigration attorneys drowning in documentation.
- Universities juggling international student paperwork.
- Executives from multinational corporations.
- Adoption facilitators with global branches.
- Relocation gurus and travel fixers.
- Regular folks with family abroad and no clue where to begin.

And guess what? Most of these people are flying blind. They're looking for a specialist. Someone who can say, "**Don't worry, I got this**." That someone can be you.

Your Workflow: The Apostille Playbook

Let's untangle how to run a client's apostille job from start to finish:

Step 1: Document Check. Figure out if the document needs notarization. Vital records like death or birth certificates often don't, but always verify.

Step 2: Notarize (If Required). If needed, conduct a standard notarization with zero margin for error. Sloppy here equals rejected later.

Step 3: Pinpoint the Destination. You must know where the document's heading is. Hague Convention countries accept apostilles; others, like China, may demand full-on embassy legalization.

Step 4: Submit to the Secretary of State. Either walk it in if your state allows, or mail it with the proper request form, check, and prayers for no delays.

Step 5: Return the Magic. Once the apostille is issued, get it into the client's hands or off to its foreign address, pronto.

Federal vs. State Apostilles

Most documents get apostilled through your state's Secretary of State. But when it comes to federal documents like FBI background checks or patent filings, you're dealing with the U.S. Department of State in Washington, D.C.

You have options:

- Offer the federal service yourself (expect delays), or
- Link up with a reliable D.C. processing agency and act as the go-between.
- Office of Notary Commission:
- 899 North Capitol St NE, Suite #8100
- Washington, DC 20002
- (202) 727-3117 www,Notary@dc,gov

Must Have Tools of the Trade

To play in this league, you'll need:

- A solid printer and scanner.
- Current apostille request forms (state and federal).
- A working knowledge of Hague vs. non-Hague countries.
- Contracts, intake forms, and shipping supplies.
- A website or landing page that looks professional.

Marketing Prompt: Tailor it to fit your business

"Craft a professional introduction for a notary offering Apostille services to various sectors, including law firms, universities, multinational companies, executives, adoption agencies, travel and relocation consultants, and individuals with families overseas. Highlight the importance of an Apostille in authenticating documents for international use. Explain the benefits of using these services, such as efficiency, expertise, and compliance with international laws. Encourage potential clients to reach out for tailored solutions to their specific needs, and emphasize commitment to excellence and customer satisfaction in facilitating smooth document processing for any international transaction."

Pro Tips for Success

- **Offer Rush and Same Day Options**: Charge a premium for speed.
- **Bundle Services**: Include notarization, apostille, and shipping.
- **Be Clear:** Explain what you can and can't do. Some clients may think you can issue an apostille directly.
- **Stay Informed:** Rules change. Bookmark your state's official apostille page and check regularly. Search the NNA website http://www.nationalnotary.org
- **Track Everything:** This goes without saying. Always log dates, tracking numbers, and document types.

Apostille services allow you to build an international business without leaving your zip code. You help people send love, business, and opportunity across borders, all while making a healthy profit.

The best part? Once you learn the system, it becomes **repeatable and scalable**. You can train others, hire couriers, or partner with immigration professionals to grow.

As you can see by now, there are numerous ways to exponentially boost your notary license with Apostille services. However, this requires thorough research, specialized training, and unwavering dedication. It's highly beneficial to seek out a mentor if possible, as their guidance can be invaluable. Don't hesitate to contact the NNA with all your questions. They are a great resource. Becoming a member can streamline this process significantly. If you set up this aspect of your business correctly from the very beginning, you'll be well on your way to becoming that $11,000 a month notary in no time, achieving financial freedom, flexibility, and professional fulfillment.

CHAPTER 4

Live Scan Fingerprinting

Key Notes:

The Four F's

Finance, Freedom, Flexibility, Family

If you're a notary public ready to evolve with demand, Live Scan fingerprinting isn't optional; it's essential. This is where precision tech meets real-world need, and those who adapt early grab the lion's share of an uncrowded market.

What Exactly Is Live Scan Fingerprinting?

Live Scan is a biometric identification method that captures fingerprints digitally and transmits them to agencies like the DOJ or FBI for background screenings. It replaces outdated ink and paper techniques with secure, real-time submission.

This service is mandatory for:

- Employment checks: pharmacy techs, funeral planners, healthcare aides
- State-regulated licensing: nurses, teachers, dental professionals, guards
- Immigration, visas, or DOJ record reviews
- Professional accreditation: notaries, CPAs, real estate agents
- Volunteer clearances: foster care, adoption, childcare
- Legal filings: expungement, identity correction

By offering this service, you become an indispensable part of how people work, travel, adopt, teach, serve, and secure legal rights.

Why Add Live Scan to Your Business Toolbox?

Here's why notaries who offer fingerprinting stay booked:

- **Consistent volume**: Licensing boards and employers send people in waves
- **Lucrative appointments**: Average revenue per scan ranges from $25 to $90 plus

- **Light competition**: Especially outside major metros
- **Same people, extra service**: Notary clients often need prints too
- **Bulk business**: Clinics, schools, and law offices need 10 to 100 prints at a time
- **Expandable**: Hire fingerprint techs or add machines to service new zones

Some notaries pull five figures monthly with no flashy website, no paid ads, just trust and repetition.

Becoming a Certified Live Scan Technician

Rules vary by state, but most follow the same core path. Let's use California as an example:

Start With an Application:

- File the Request for Live Scan Certification with the California DOJ
- Clear a background check
- Show proof of experience or complete training, even YouTube counts, but classroom learning wins credibility

Gear You Will Need:

- Digital fingerprint scanner $1,500 to $4,000
- Encryption-compliant software license
- Computer or laptop
- Portable cart if offering mobile appointments

Vendors like IDEMIA and Futronic sell the scanners. DOJ-approved software is essential, and depending on your tech savvy, an IT install pro might be your first worthwhile hire.

Live Scan Is More Than an Add-On, It's an Advantage

The fingerprinting industry is built on trust, regulation, and urgency. That's exactly where notaries shine. With a few upgrades and a shift in mindset, you're not only notarizing, you're securing identities, enabling careers, and meeting urgent compliance deadlines.

And best of all: while others are still passing business cards, you're processing $700 worth of scans at a job fair.

This is your moment. Keep your notary seal, but power it up with prints.

https://na.idemia.com/

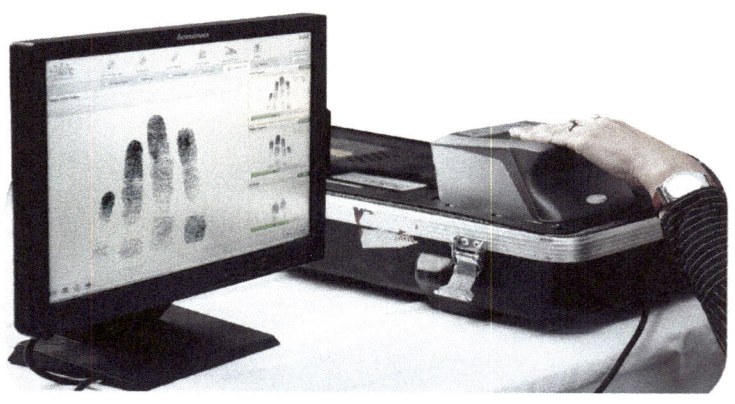

http://futronictech.com

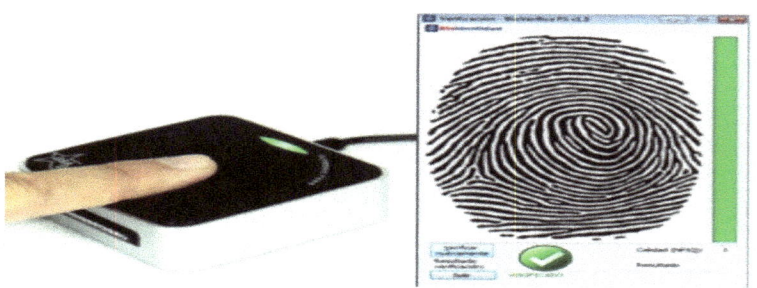

To run a legitimate and secure Live Scan business, you must establish a dependable infrastructure. This includes:

- Encrypted systems with locked-down password protocols
- Uninterrupted and stable internet connection
- Transparent, well-documented record-keeping procedures
- Data transmission methods that meet legal encryption and privacy standards

Note: Certain states may dispatch regulatory agents to audit your setup. If you're not in compliance, you're off the list.

Once cleared, your enterprise is listed in your state's official Live Scan vendor directory, your digital storefront where clients locate and reach out to you directly.

Fee Breakdown: What You Can Earn

Fingerprinting charges are composed of:

- Your personal rolling fee
- Government-imposed DOJ and FBI background check fees

Rolling fees generally range from $25 to $50. Once you include the agency processing cost, total client charges hover between $50 and $90 or more. Your margin lives in the rolling fee and any additional premiums, such as travel surcharges.

Sample Income Scenarios:

- 10 clients × $35 = $350 per day
- 20 clients at a hiring event × $35 = $700 in a single day

Educational institutions and HR departments yield high volume, repeat business. That's where your numbers grow.

Who Uses Live Scan Services?

Your key clientele includes:

- Public and private schools: teachers, teaching aides, admin staff
- Security services: guards, supervisors, field agents
- Real estate: brokers, agents, leasing consultants
- Healthcare: doctors, nurses, support techs
- Nonprofits: volunteers in child and elder care programs
- Government: agency employees and outside contractors
- Law offices: clients filing for background record updates or expungements

Look for sectors that recruit consistently. These are your reliable repeat buyers.

Going Mobile: Where the Money Moves

Too many Live Scan professionals confine themselves to a single location. That limits your income. Portability creates opportunity.

Take your Live Scan gear directly to:

- Job fairs
- Corporate buildings
- Professional conferences
- K12 and higher education campuses
- Hospitals and private clinics
- State licensing events

Add an on-site fee of $25 to $75 per client. Group bookings reduce your cost and increase your output. A mobile-only Live Scan setup is not just doable; it thrives especially in regions lacking walk-in facilities.

Attracting Clients: Build a Business That Gets Booked

You want to be visible, dependable, and trusted. Start here:

1. Website Must-Haves

- Highlight Live Scan as your core service
- Embed a seamless booking interface
- Clarify what clients must bring (ID, fees, etc.)
- List approved agencies and accepted submission types
- Show mobile service zones

2. Outreach Strategy

- Partner with:
- Real estate education programs
- Beauty and barber licensing academies
- Nursing colleges and training centers
- Technical or trade schools

Offer group rates or organize on-campus fingerprinting days for convenience and visibility.

Real Case: Sandra's Six-Figure Side Hustle

Maritza, a notary from California, added Live Scan in her second year. By year three:

- She was the go-to provider for three school districts
- Served local nursing schools weekly
- Charged $35 per scan, handling 20 to 30 per day

Her fingerprinting alone now generates over $110,000 annually with less than 20 work hours per week. She built a lean, high-earning model from scratch.

Sidebar: Massive Market Size Equals Massive Opportunity

Numbers don't lie:

- 71,000 plus concealed carry permits in California

- 11 million plus permit holders across the U.S.

- 325,000 plus active nurses in California

- 5.6 million plus nurses nationwide

- 200,000 plus licensed Realtors in California

- Over 3 million real estate professionals nationwide

Every single one of them needs fingerprinting. If you're listening closely, you might hear that cash register starting to chirp.

Live Scan isn't just another service. It's a sharp alignment with today's compliance-heavy environment. Whether you're using digital biometric devices or traditional fingerprint rollers, this avenue upgrades your notary business and meets a demand that won't disappear.

And the best part? You already have the license. Now, it's time to make it work harder for you.

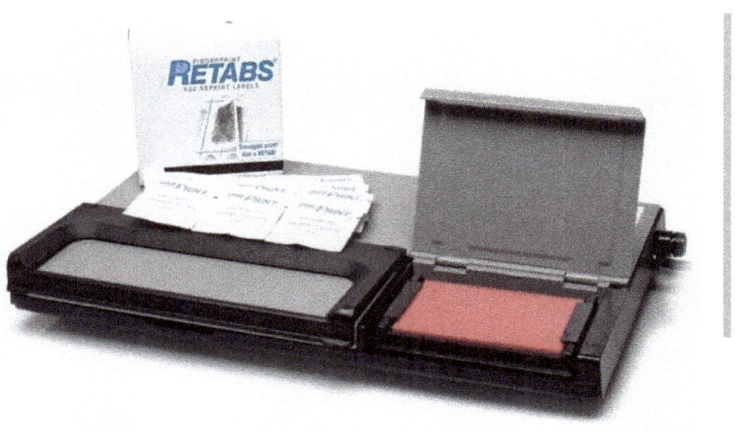

It's people-focused and absolutely scalable.

You don't need to abandon notary work; you're just building new income on top of it.

CHAPTER 5

Jail Signing Services

Key Notes:

The Four F's

Finance, Freedom, Flexibility, Family

When people envision notarial tasks, their minds usually conjure images of neat desks, corporate folders, and crisp paper shuffles. Yet hidden behind the curtain lies a powerful, urgent, and often ignored niche: jail notary work. It's a lane of service where immediacy meets humanity, and most overlook it.

Your worth as a notary extends far beyond embossed seals and witness lines. You are a bridge to justice, especially when justice resides behind locked steel and cement.

Inside lockups, access is everything. And where there is a barrier, there's a notary like you cutting through it.

What is Jail Signing Services:

Harold at www.NotaryBuilder.com is a major resource.

Jail signings involve meeting incarcerated individuals inside detention centers to notarize pressing legal or personal documents.

These are the usual suspects:

- Power of Attorney (POA) assignments
- Custody transfers or parental designations
- Real estate paperwork, such as grant deeds or refinancing forms
- Consent forms for child travel, medical decisions, or school registration
- Immigration affidavits
- Business management or dissolution documents
- Personal declarations or sworn statements

Each document carries serious consequences. Some carry tears. All carry urgency. You become the person who grants them legitimacy.

Why This Niche Matters Deeply

Here's what sets this service apart:

- **Urgency equals leverage.** These documents can't wait. Families will often pay top-tier prices to meet tight deadlines.
- **Low saturation.** Few notaries want to navigate steel gates and concrete blocks. That leaves you with fewer rivals.
- **Client recurrence.** Attorneys, relatives, and bondsmen often return with repeat needs or send others your way.
- **Meaningful impact.** These signings don't just authorize paperwork. They reunite families, protect rights, and shape destinies.

You're not stamping papers. You're anchoring people.

Launching Your Jail Notary Services

Step One: Learn the Institution's Protocol

Every correctional center has its own rulebook. Some welcome notaries with scheduled visits. Others demand thorough background vetting or administrative clearance.

Make these calls in advance:

- Do notaries get access?
- What identification must the inmate present?
- Must I be listed on the inmate's visitor log?
- Are there restricted hours for document signings?
- May I carry writing tools or a notary ledger inside?
- Is there secure storage for personal items?

Be steady, courteous, and clear. Building relationships with jail staff opens doors faster than any badge.

Step Two: Aim Your Outreach Intelligently

You're not marketing to the jailhouse. You're connecting with:

- Families of incarcerated individuals
- Defense and family law attorneys
- Bail bond agents
- Nonprofit case managers or social workers
- Motorcycle club members with incarcerated brothers
- You'll locate them via:
- Search engine campaigns targeting jail notary near me
- Paper ads in courthouses, attorney lobbies, or bail offices
- Strategic alliances with immigration law offices or family legal reps
- Local digital forums or neighborhood-based Facebook groups
- Collaboration with prisoner aid programs or reentry projects

Suggested Message:

Delivering notary services inside detention centers isn't about stamps. It's about reliability when it counts. If you're a legal advocate, bail agent, social worker, or support network, my jail signing service simplifies the hardest part of getting it done. I show up on site, with speed and respect, and handle your client's urgent paperwork face-to-face. No confusion. No delay. Let's connect to help your clients navigate the pressure with precision.

Marketing Prompt: Tailor it to fit your needs

Create a dynamic marketing message for notaries specializing in jail signing services aimed at companies and individuals like criminal and family lawyers, bail bond companies, social workers, travel agencies, and motorcycle clubs. Highlight the convenience and accessibility of on-site jail signing, emphasizing reliability, speed, and professionalism. Describe how these services enhance client satisfaction and facilitate urgent legal processes. Include a strong call to action encouraging potential partners to reach out for collaboration, showcasing your commitment to helping them and their clients navigate complex situations with ease and expertise."

Step Three: Structure Your Rates with Confidence

Correctional signings aren't ordinary. Your time, effort, and unique access deserve premium pay.

Here's a common price tier:

- **Travel and Visit Fee:** $100 to $200, depending on distance and security levels
- **Wait Fee:** First 30 minutes included. After that, $1 to $2 per minute
- **Per Signature Fee:** Based on your state's notarial regulations
- **Off-Hour Appointments:** Additional charge for weekends, holidays, or late-night slots

Clients usually don't flinch. They know these documents are make-or-break.

Example Breakdown:

- 30-mile trip: $150
- 40-minute wait: (10 minutes paid) $10
- 2 notarization document signings $30

- **Total: $190**

Plenty of notaries report making $250 to $400 for a single jail run. I often offer a discount on repeat visits, especially when the signing is quick and hassle-free.

Your Jail Signing Essentials

Carry:

- Valid government ID
- Business card
- Notary journal and 2 working pens
- Relevant paperwork, which is usually provided by family or a lawyer
- Composure. Delays are frequent. Patience is your best asset.
- Leave behind:
- Mobile phone, many jails restrict or ban them
- Non-essential personal items
- Any documents not pre-approved by jail staff

You might be subject to pat-downs or long wait times. Once, I had to stand outside a watchtower for over 30 minutes until an officer could come down and escort me inside. Always stay professional.

Tips for Effective Jail Notary Work

- **Stay agile:** Confirm all appointments. Lockdowns happen without warning.
- **Encourage loyalty:** Offer small gestures for referrals, like a thank-you discount or gas card.
- **Communicate post-signing:** A quick follow-up reassures families

and builds rapport.

- **Package services:** Offer to scan, deliver, or file documents for an added fee.

- **Be humane:** These are stressful situations. Speak gently and carry dignity in your voice.

True Story: $5K Month from Jail Signings

Thomas, a notary working out of San Diego, got into jail signings to help a buddy. Six months later, he was:

- On speed dial for three attorneys

- A regular face at two bail agencies

- Fielding calls weekly for POAs, custody papers, and declarations

He charges $175 per trip and logs around 5 to 8 visits per week.

Monthly income from jail jobs alone: $4,500 to $6,000.

His success recipe? Consistency. Kindness. And knowing jail procedures like the back of his hand.

Protect Yourself in High-Stress Settings

Your well-being outranks everything. Stay sharp by:

- Letting someone know where you're headed
- Sharing your location through a tracker app
- Remaining calm in tense or emotional settings
- Trusting your gut. If something doesn't feel right, leave

Most jail visits go smoothly. In eight years, I've only experienced one lockdown triggered by an inmate scuffle. Ninety-nine percent of detainees are calm, respectful, and deeply grateful.

People behind bars are still people. They deserve connection, rights, and a second chance. Many are trying to fix what went wrong. And often, you're the person who hands them the pen to start.

Jail notary services aren't simply a business.

They're an act of decency. A service to society. And a rare opportunity to do meaningful work while earning an honest income.

When you walk into a jail with your briefcase and badge, you're not just a notary.

You're a witness to resilience. A provider of peace. And sometimes, the only open door in a locked building.

CHAPTER 6

Working with Bail Bonds Companies

Key Notes:

The Four F's

Finance, Freedom, Flexibility, Family

You've grasped the firepower behind jail signings. Now shift your focus to another overlooked goldmine that yields fast, steady income for the sharp notary: **Bail Bond Partnerships**.

This isn't theory. This is experience. I've walked both lanes as a licensed notary and a working bail bond agent for over eight years. This chapter isn't fluff. It's the blueprint. Read every line like your next check depends on it.

Every single day, arrests happen. Families go into panic mode. The bail process begins, often after dark and under pressure. That process frequently depends on notarized signatures, is fast, legal, and has no room for error.

This chapter will show you what bail bondsmen do, where you come in, how to pitch your value, and how to turn one-off visits into ongoing cash flow.

Also, in chapter eleven, you will find forms that you'll need to become familiar with.

Bail Bonds Business: A Quick Breakdown

When someone's cuffed, the judge may set bail. This bail is money held to guarantee the accused returns to court.

Most people don't have the money on hand, so they go to a bail bond agency.

The agency posts the full bail for a non-refundable fee, usually 7% to 10% of the full bond amount. To secure this, they often require a cosigner and sometimes collateral, like a vehicle or home. This whole process triggers a chain of paperwork, and here's your cue. When a home is used as collateral, the surety company will require a Deed of Trust. This is where the big bucks start to roll in.

Get familiar with the Deed of Trust document. Each surety company will have different required forms.

Common notarial tasks:

- Indemnity contracts: making the cosigner liable
- Powers of attorney: empowering agents to act on behalf of the accused
- Collateral documents: securing assets against the bond
- Payment plans
- Jail release paperwork
- Deed of Trust and security agreements

Why Bail Notary Work Pays Fast and Big

I stumbled into this niche quite unexpectedly. I was notarizing some documents for a police officer, a friend of mine, when we began an informal discussion about his side job. He worked as a recovery agent for bail bond companies. In passing, he mentioned that these companies frequently required notaries when he was in the process of surrendering someone. Think "Dog The Bounty Hunter," if you will. Allow me to clarify.

When an individual willfully neglects to show up for a mandated court date, they can be charged with 'Failure to Appear,' according to California Penal Codes 1320 and 1320.5. Upon this action, the judge will issue an official bench warrant, and law enforcement, or in our case, bounty hunters, will promptly arrive at your doorstep.

If these bounty hunters fail to locate you and return you to court within 30 days, the bail bond company stands to lose a substantial sum. This is where the necessity for collateral comes in, and this is where you, as the notary, can generate a tidy sum working with bail bond companies.

Consider it akin to a loan gone bad, or a house falling out of escrow. Understanding why this is so crucial becomes apparent when a bond exceeds $200,000. The surety or insurance carrier backing the bail bond company typically demands collateral. In most instances, this tends to be a home with sufficient equity to cover the entire bond. Certified loan signing agents thrive in this scenario, as the documents bear striking similarities to their field of expertise. Imagine a Deed of Trust, but tailored to the bail bonds industry. This is precisely why notaries play a pivotal role, securing the asset swiftly and accurately.

Once a bail bond agent develops a level of comfort with a notary well-versed in this area, they're likely to recommend them to every notary they know. I will provide an example using travel expenses, but do remember, a flat fee structure tends to work best with this type of notarization.

Bail agents don't mess around. They need responsive notaries who answer calls and move with urgency.

Example Pay Structure:

- Travel: $75 to $150 depending on location
- After hours: Add $50 for evenings, weekends, or holidays
- Signatures: $10 to $25 each
- Wait Time: $1to $2 per minute after 15 to 30 minutes

Real Example:

- 8:30 PM appointment
- Two docs
- 20-minute wait
- Invoice:
- $100 travel
- $50 after hours
- $20 signatures
- $10 wait
- **Total: $180**

I round it off and charge $200 for all Deed of Trust signings, no matter the distance traveled. With solid connections, you can run 2 of these in a single night. I operate across four office locations with over 15 active bail agents. One productive bail agent alone can fill up your weekly calendar.

Why This Lane Deserves Your Focus

- High volume: Some agents handle 10 plus clients daily
- Time sensitive equals premium pricing
- Repeat jobs: Agents stick with those they trust
- Quick turnaround: Most signings wrap in 30 minutes
- Upsell potential: Jail visits, scanning, delivery service, POA prep

Once you prove yourself, you're their go-to. They won't shop for another notary. You're locked in.

How to Lock In Bail Bond Partners

Step 1: Locate Your Local Bail Agents

Use Google, Yelp, and courthouse directories to gather:

- Offices near jails and court buildings
- 24/7 agencies
- Multilingual agents (Spanish-speaking agents serve a wide demographic. I have my AA in ASL, which is an amazing niche market)

Build a hit list of 10 to 20 contacts.

Step 2: Deliver a Strong Pitch

Call or, even better, walk in.

Say something like:

"Hi, I'm [Your Name], a mobile notary who works fast, day or night. I know your business moves fast and you need legal docs signed now, not later. I've helped bail agents before, and I'm available 24/7. I'm fast, reliable, and easy to work with."

Bring:

- Business cards
- Notepads or pens with your info
- A printed one-sheet showing your services and hours
- Coffee or donuts, trust me, food opens doors faster than flyers

Step 3: Offer a Trial or Intro Discount

A first timer rate or no risk trial goes a long way. Once you show up, smile, and deliver without problems, they'll save your number.

You Might Face These Challenges

1. **Late-night or emergency calls:** Decide if you want to offer 24/7. If yes, set boundaries. If not, make your hours clear.
2. **High-pressure moments:** Families may be scared, angry, or overwhelmed. You stay calm. Be the adult in the room.
3. **Missing or messy document:** Remind agents to prep ahead. Bring clean copies of key forms likethe Deed of Trust directly from your surety.
4. **No shows:** Charge a dry run fee (non-refundable). It's standard practice in the bail industry.

Add-On Services to Boost Your Value

Once you're in, offer:

- Courier work: Drop off documents at court or law firms
- Witness sourcing: Some docs require two people present
- Scanning and digital delivery: Especially helpful for attorneys
- You're not a notary anymore. You're a legal logistics partner.

Real Success Story: $10K a Month on Bail Jobs

Marie from Los Angeles turned five bail agent relationships into a six-figure hustle. She:

- Charged $150 plus per visit
- Did 3 to 4 jobs daily
- Worked 20-plus gigs a week

All referral-based. No ads. No gimmicks. Her secret weapon? Fast replies, no cancellations, and bringing fresh donuts.

Important Legal and Ethical Notes

- Do not give legal advice. Ever.
- Don't promise anything about the defendant's release.
- Always verify IDs.
- Keep a detailed journal. I've had a police call about entries. Your records protect you.
- Know your state's specific notary rules around bail bonds.

This is a Serious Opportunity

Working with bail bond companies turns your notary business from a side gig into a serious income channel.

You reconnect families. You keep legal timelines intact. And you earn handsomely for stepping up when others are asleep.

All it takes is one relationship to change everything.

Don't treat this chapter lightly. You wouldn't ignore a winning lotto ticket. Don't ignore this either. Here is my direct email: fastfreddie2727@gmail.com for any questions.

This is your Microsoft stock moment.

BONUS

Want to work with sureties? Here are three major ones:

1. Bankers Insurance Company
11101 Roosevelt Blvd N, St. Petersburg, FL 33716

(727) 823-4000
http://bankersinsurance.com

2. Financial Casualty & Surety, Inc.

3131 Eastside Street, Suite 250, Houston, TX 77098(877) 737-2245
www.fcsurety.com

3. United States Fire Insurance Company

157 Main Street, Greenville, PA 16125
(800) 245-0366 Fax (724) 588-8801
Email: CourtNotices@cfins.com

Email Template:

Hi, my name is [**Your Name**]. I'm a notary in [**Your State**] and I work closely with bail bond companies. Can you email me the current Deed of Trust packet your company uses for collateral on bonds?

Thank you,[Your Name and Contact Information]

CHAPTER 7

Mobile Notary Service

Key Notes:

The Four F's

Finance, Freedom, Flexibility, Family

In today's fast-paced world, people want services delivered where they are, whether at home, work, or a coffee shop. That's why **mobile notary services** are one of the most in-demand and scalable ways to make money with your notary commission.

If you can drive, keep a schedule, and act professionally, you can build a six-figure mobile notary business. All it takes is smart marketing, excellent customer service, and a commitment to being the most reliable option in town.

In this chapter, we'll break down the nuts and bolts of mobile notary work, how to set yourself apart, where to find clients, and how to scale this into a dominant local brand.

What Are Mobile Notary Services?

A **mobile notary** travels to clients to perform notarizations. Instead of them coming to your office, you go to them at their home, job, hospital room, café even gentlemen's clubs.

Documents commonly notarized by mobile notaries include:

- Real estate forms
- Power of Attorney
- Trusts and wills
- Healthcare directives
- Affidavits and letters
- Business contracts
- School and medical paperwork
- Divorce and custody forms

This service is all about **convenience** and **accessibility**, two things people will gladly pay a premium for.

Why Mobile Notary Work Is a Goldmine

Mobile notary work is one of the most flexible and profitable paths:

- **You set the schedule:** Work full-time, part-time, evenings, weekends, whatever suits your lifestyle.
- **Minimal overhead**: You don't need an office. Just your notary kit and a car.
- **Endless demand:** Individuals, families, attorneys, title companies, nursing homes, and more need mobile notaries daily.
- **Premium pricing:** People pay for convenience, especially in emergencies.

How to Build Your Mobile Notary Business

Step 1: Choose Your Service Area

Start with a realistic driving radius, 10 to 25 miles is typical. Remember, time is money. Consider:

- Population density
- Traffic and parking
- Areas underserved by other notaries

Pro tip: Start with your **home zip code** and maybe your closest downtown business district, then expand based on demand.

Step 2: Get the Right Tools

Your mobile notary essentials:

- Notary journal
- Stamp and embossing seal
- Reliable pen (blue and black)
- Two forms of your own ID

- Clipboard or signing surface
- GPS and phone charger
- Optional: Portable scanner or printer for real estate signings

Step 3: Set Your Prices

Pricing should reflect your experience, the document complexity, and your travel range. Check with your state and the NNA for notary travel fee rules and guidelines.

Typical fees:

- **Travel Fee**: $50 to $150 depending on distance and time
- **Notarization Fee**: State maximum per signature (often $10 to $15)
- **After Hours or Emergency Fee**: plus $25 to $100
- **Wait Time**: Free first 15 minutes, then $1 to $2 per minute

Example:
Client calls at 8 PM for a POA at their home, 10 miles away. You charge:

- $75 travel
- $15 notarization
- $25 late fee
  Total: $115 for a 30-minute visit.

How to Get Clients and Keep Them

1. Build a Strong Online Presence

Your website and profiles: Key Words SEO: I'm available. I'm a professional. I'm fast.

- **Google Business Profile:** Show up in local searches. Ask clients for reviews!
- **Yelp and Thumbtack:** People use these to find notaries on

demand.

- **Your own website:** Include services, pricing, testimonials, and contact info.

Pro tip: Post regularly on social media about real-life signings. The crazier or funnier, the better. (with client consent, of course).

2. Network Locally

Become the first name people think of when they need a notary. Build relationships with:

- Law offices
- Real estate agents
- Nursing homes
- Hospitals
- Local banks and credit unions
- Title and escrow officers
- Small business owners

Bring cards, offer free consultations, and follow up after your first visit. Don't forget the donuts and free giveaways. Trust me, this really works.

MARKETING PROMPT: Tailor to fit your needs

"Develop a concise marketing strategy for mobile notaries targeting law offices, real estate agents, nursing homes, hospitals, local banks, credit unions, title and escrow officers, and small business owners. Emphasize the benefits of quick reliable, and cost-effective notary services that enhance convenience and efficiency for clients. Highlight flexible scheduling and travel capabilities to accommodate busy professionals. Create promotional materials that include clear messaging, compelling visuals, and a strong call to action encouraging potential clients to contact you for immediate service needs, Focus on building relationships and trust within the community through exceptional service."

3. Be Hyper Responsive

Speed is everything in mobile notary work. Many clients call 3 to 5 notaries and go with whoever answers first.

- Use call forwarding or an answering service if you're busy.
- Reply to texts or emails quickly and professionally.
- Confirm appointments and give ETAs.

The faster you respond, the more jobs you'll book.

What Makes a Great Mobile Notary?

Success in this business isn't about being flashy. It's about being:

- **Reliable:** Always show up on time
- **Clear:** Explain what's happening and what's needed
- **Respectful:** Clients may be elderly, grieving, or stressed
- **Professional:** Dress well, speak clearly, and act like a service provider
- **Prepared**: Double-check documents, IDs, and requirements

Your job is to **make their life easier**. If you do that, they'll refer you over and over.

Add-On Services to Increase Your Earnings

Offer additional services to increase your average ticket:

- **Printing and delivery of documents**
- **Courier drop-off to FedEx/UPS/attorney**
- **Remote Online Notary (RON)** offers online options for certain clients

You can even bundle services into packages like:

- Estate Plan Signing: POA plus Will

- New Parent Package: Guardianship plus School Authorization
- Senior Care Package: Living Trust plus Healthcare Directive

CHAPTER 8

Power of
Attorney

Key Notes:

The Four F's

Finance, Freedom, Flexibility, Family

Power of Attorney (POA) documents rank among the most delicate and high-stakes legal instruments a notary will ever confront. These authorizations assign consequential decision-making powers. Financial, medical, and legal issues from one individual to another. They are not routine papers; they are lifelines etched in ink.

Facilitating a POA signing isn't a task. It's a position of solemn trust and precision. It pays well, but more importantly, it demands an unshakable devotion to correctness. Overlooking a detail in this process could spiral into legal entanglements for everyone involved. This chapter scrutinizes POA variants, pinpoints procedural essentials, outlines the perils, and illustrates how you can earn credibility and income in this pivotal area.

Comprehending the Nature of Power of Attorney

A Power of Attorney is a formal delegation where the principal entrusts an individual, the agent or attorney-in-fact, with the authority to act on their behalf. These forms vary widely in scope and implication. Misidentifying their type isn't a small error. It's a fracture in professional responsibility.

Types of POA Instruments:

1. General POA: Grants unrestrained power across financial and legal domains.

2. Special or Limited POA: Restricts authority to specific matters, such as real estate transactions or account management.

3. Durable POA: Remains enforceable even after the principal loses mental capacity.

4. Springing POA: Dormant until a triggering event, often cognitive decline or incapacitation.

5. Medical POA: Transfers healthcare decision-making authority once the principal is unable to do so.

Why POA Signings Demand Notarial Oversight

Numerous jurisdictions stipulate notarization for a POA to be valid. Even where not mandated, banks, medical institutions, and legal systems often insist on notarized validation.

Your function provides:

- Formal authentication
- Assurance to all parties involved
- Tangible proof of identity and willingness

Typical clientele:

- Seniors arranging end-of-life affairs
- Families bracing for medical unknowns
- Professionals or military personnel facing travel or deployment
- Entrepreneurs needing financial delegation

Your Position in the Legal Framework

As a notary, you're not an adjudicator of legal merit. You don't interpret or validate the content. Your mission:

- Confirm the signer's identity
- Observe their mental clarity
- Confirm their voluntary participation
- Complete your journal and seal impeccably

Stay alert for warning signs:

- A signer who appears dazed, medicated, or manipulated
- A family member overtaking the conversation
- Documents that are incomplete or suspicious

If any part feels compromised, disengage. You hold the right to walk away.

The POA Signing Process: Step-by-Step

1. Clarify Statutory Obligations

   - Some states demand two disinterested witnesses alongside notarization

   - Ensure you comprehend ID laws and document requirements

2. Check Documents and Credentials

   - Scrutinize for errors, blanks, or mismatched names

   - Validate the person listed is indeed the principal

3. Gauge Mental Acuity

   - Ask direct questions: Do you understand this authorization?

   - Be wary of silence, confusion, or a blank stare

4. Observe the Signature

   - Signer must ink their name in your direct presence

   - Witnesses must do the same, if applicable

5. Seal the Transaction

   - Complete your notarial certificate meticulously

   - Use your seal, sign, and record diligently

6. Offer Value-Added Services

   - Scan and forward to attorneys or family

   - Provide duplicate originals

   - Deliver documents to banks, hospitals, or law offices

Promoting Your POA Services Strategically

POA services are intimate and irreplaceable. People seek professionals with composure, tact, and discretion.

Position yourself as:

- Competent
- Compassionate
- Informed
- Discreet

Proven Marketing Techniques:

1. Forge Ties with Elder Law Experts

   - Offer on-location visits for their clientele
   - Develop flyers or one-pagers outlining your POA process
   - Provide emergency access, including weekends

2. Connect with Care Institutions

   - Assisted living, rehab centers, and memory care units frequently require mobile notaries
   - Offer discounted group sessions or recurring availability
   - Build rapport with facility staff and caseworkers

3. Educate the General Public

   - Produce quick, informative video clips or articles explaining POAs
   - Promote these around national estate planning observances

Marketing Script Sample for Brochures or Flyers:

You deliver an essential service to elders and their families. You protect their intent. You ensure decisions about money and medical care reflect their will. Your brochure must radiate professionalism, empathy, and readiness. Mention your mobility, your 24/7 availability, and your background. Include brief testimonials to enhance credibility and convert readers into clients.

PROMPT FOR POA MARKETING:

"Create a compelling brochure or one-sheet for notaries specializing in Power of Attorney services, targeting senior centers, assisted living facilities, elder law attorneys, estate planners, hospitals, and nursing homes. Emphasize professionalism, compassion, knowledge, and confidence in providing essential legal services for seniors. Include key benefits of having a power of attorney, such as ensuring medical and financial decisions are handled according to the client's wishes. Highlight your experience, availability for on-site services, and commitment to supporting families during difficult transitions. Incorporate testimonials or case studies to build trust and encourage potential clients to reach out for personalized consultation."

Suggested Compensation Structure

People do not hesitate to pay for certainty when lives and assets hang in the balance.

Service Fees: Sample Ranges
Check your state guidelines.

- Travel surcharge: $50 to $150

- Per-signature fee: $10 to $25

- Coordinating impartial witnesses: $25 to $50

- After hours and urgent signings: $25 to $75 additional

- Printing or document prep: $10 to $20

Common Earnings per Session: $85 to $200, with some engagements exceeding $300 based on complexity and urgency.

Shielding Yourself from Liability

POAs can invite intense legal scrutiny. Avoid missteps with airtight practices:

- Meticulously log every interaction in your journal

- Record ID information without exception

- If unsure of the signer's awareness or free will, delay or decline

- Secure Errors & Omissions coverage (minimum $50,000 advised)

Never let pressure, guilt, or urgency compromise your integrity. Refusing a notarization might save your license or a family's fortune.

Real Life Lesson: When Saying No Saves Everything

Jeanette, a Las Vegas-based mobile notary, responded to a call for a Durable POA signing in a rehabilitation facility. Upon arrival, she found the principal non-verbal and likely medicated. The daughter insisted her father was lucid and aware.

Jeanette, holding firm to ethical boundaries, refused to notarize. Days later, that same daughter attempted to use a falsified POA to seize property assets. Jeanette's refusal spared her from a potential legal nightmare.

Your discernment doesn't merely protect you. It safeguards families, generational wealth, and reputations.

The True Weight of the Signature

Being present for a POA signing is more than procedural. It's a moment where your pen affirms a person's voice, even when they may not speak for themselves later.

Learn the laws. Refine your approach. Stay vigilant. Earn trust. Do this, and you will become not only a sought-after expert but a meaningful part of your community's legal safety net. And you will be paid for your diligence, judgment, and principled presence.

MAKE A DIFFERENCE WHILE HAVING A PURPOSE.

CHAPTER 9

Remote Online Notarization (RON)

Key Notes:

The Four F's

Finance, Freedom, Flexibility, Family

As the world shifts toward convenience and virtual access, Remote Online Notarization (RON) is swiftly ascending as an elite and lucrative arena for notaries craving autonomy and scalability. Gone are the days of geographical confines. Your notary reach can now transcend state lines, international borders, and time zones, all orchestrated from your home setup.

With RON, you officiate legal signings through encrypted video sessions. Your client might be five blocks away or on another continent. The ink is digital. The distance is irrelevant. If you're pivoting to amplify your reach, diminish travel fatigue, or build a virtual notary practice with teeth, RON is your runway.

Dissecting Remote Online Notarization

Remote Online Notarization permits commissioned notaries to authenticate documents via live, secure video transmission. Instead of conventional handshakes and office chairs, RON sessions unfold in secure cyber rooms where identity is validated, sessions are recorded, and digital seals are affixed.

What comprises a RON session:

- Biometric and data-driven ID validation via credential checks and knowledge-based interrogation
- Full audiovisual archive of the meeting
- Tamper-evident electronic signatures and notary stamps

The legal footprint of RON is expanding rapidly throughout the U.S., fueled by both necessity and modernity post-pandemic. More states are codifying it. More industries are embracing it.

How RON Departs from Its Predecessors

Category	Traditional Notarization	Mobile Notarization	RON
Physicality	In person only	You drive to them	Online portal
Signature Type	Pen on paper	Pen on paper	Digital
ID Check	Eyeball inspection	Eyeball inspection	Layered digital scrutiny
Tools	Logbook & stamp	Logbook & stamp	Webcam, platform credentials
Session Record	No recording	No recording	Recorded
Access	Fixed schedule	Travel dependent	24/7 digital storefront

RON serves:

- Transient professionals
- Bedridden individuals or quarantined parties
- Globalized teams
- Overseas U.S. citizens

Starting Gate: What You Need to Launch in RON

1. Live in a RON Compatible State
Not all states are enlightened yet. Over 45 have some variant of RON laws. Check your Secretary of State's page or consult the National Notary Association.

2. Secure State Level RON Certification
Steps typically include:

- A vetted RON curriculum
- Passing a digital competency exam
- Applying for a digital notary endorsement
- Procuring a valid electronic seal and certificate

3. Select Your Battlefield: RON Tech Platforms

Your notarization battlefield will be online platforms that offer encrypted video, storage, and compliance. Top contenders:

- DocVerify
- eNotaryLog
- Notarize
- Signix
- Nexsys
- OneNotary
- BlueNotary
- Pavaso (real estate)

These platforms generally cover:

- Identity validation
- Video hosting
- Document archiving
- E-journal management
- Fee structures: subscription, per use, or hybrid

4. Tech Arsenal Requirements

- Robust, wired internet
- Stable desktop or laptop
- 1080p webcam, high fidelity microphone
- Distraction-free digital workspace

Monetizing Your RON Skills

RON assignments often command steeper rates than in-person signings. States permitting tech upcharges add more padding.

Common fee structure:

- Primary RON fee: $25 to $35 per seal (state contingent)
- Platform fee: $5 to $15
- Added seals: $10 to $25 each
- Night owl or rush surcharge: $15 to $50
- Complex signings: $75 to $200 plus

Example: A New York real estate POA at midnight.

- RON: $35
- Tech and late-night fee: $20
- Platform toll: $10
  Total: $65 for fifteen focused minutes.

Multiply that by a law firm's caseload and you see the goldmine.

Where to Attract RON Clients

1. Enlist with RON Platforms
These platforms often supply a steady clientele across real estate, legal, and corporate sectors.

2. Online Presence is Mandatory
Strategically promote through:

- A sleek website
- Google Business Profile
- Posts on LinkedIn, Facebook, and Instagram
- Forums like BBB, Craigslist, and niche groups

3. Collaborate with Digital Native Enterprises
Target operations like:

- Law offices
- Tech startups
- Remote HR teams
- Offshore investors
- Online colleges

4. Service Global Americans
Expats and military households often find consulates out of reach. Your screen becomes their lifeline.

Marketing Prompt: Tailor to fit your needs

"Craft an engaging introduction for a notary offering remote online notary services targeting law firms, universities, tech startups, offshore investors, online colleges, multinational companies, travel agencies, relocation consultants, and individuals with families overseas. Highlight the convenience and security of online notarization, emphasizing compliance with legal standards and the ability to facilitate document signing from anywhere in the world. Explain how these services save time and streamline processes for busy professionals and families. Encourage potential clients to contact you for customized solutions, showcasing your commitment to exceptional service and expertise in remote notarization."

Professionalism in Practice

- Wear business attire, even if barefoot
- Opt for clean, neutral backgrounds
- Pre-check your gear religiously
- Speak slowly, guide your signer
- Encrypt and back up all records

Scaling Beyond the Ceiling

- Once fluent in RON, you accelerate:
- Multiple signings per hour
- Clients statewide or international
- Total geographic freedom
- Group appointments with ease

Case Study: From Kitchen Counter to Cross Continental

Carolyn, a Florida-based mom and notary, pivoted to RON during lockdown. She invested in high-end gear, fine-tuned her Spanish, and began serving clients across time zones.

One year in, she was grossing over $8,000 monthly without commuting. She specialized in twilight signings and Spanish-speaking clientele. Her toddler slept through prosperity.

RON Isn't a Trend. It's a Trajectory.

Remote Online Notarization is reshaping the notary landscape. With preparedness, digital fluency, and intention, your notary business transcends city blocks and enters the global chat.

Whether your aim is lifestyle autonomy or volume mastery, RON doesn't just widen your net. It hands you a much bigger ocean.

FOCUS ON THE FUTURE. REMOTE ONLINE NOTARY

Understanding the distinction between eNotarization, eSignature, and eClosing is essential for any notary looking to expand their expertise and enhance their business. As the demand for remote online notarization (RON) continues to grow, becoming proficient in these technologies is crucial. By mastering the tools and techniques of RON, you can position yourself as the go-to expert in the field. Elevate your services by offering VIP customer care, ensuring a seamless and professional experience for your clients. Embrace the future of notarization and watch your business thrive.

CHAPTER 10

Branding
And
Marketing

Key Notes:

The Four F's

Finance, Freedom, Flexibility, Family

Most notary businesses sound like someone named their company while half asleep.

ABC Notary Services
Quick Stamp Solutions
Reliable Notary 24/7
Zzzzz…

Now compare that to:

"Stamp Me Silly Notary"

"The Inkcredible Notary"

"Seal the Deal Mobile Notary"

"Notary Ninja"

Boom. People laugh. They remember. And guess what? They **CALL.**

Your brand should feel like you: bold, funny, trustworthy, and confident. Your name, slogan, and logo are your first impression. Make people feel something. Humor works. So does cleverness. You don't have to be goofy, but don't be invisible either.

Step Two: Make Social Media Your Office Assistant

Look, you don't need to dance on TikTok, unless you want to, in which case, please send me that video. But you do need to be visible.

Here's how to show up:

1. YouTube Channel: Start a series like *"Notary Knowledge Nuggets"* or "Stamp Talk with Freddie." Use your own name, of course. Keep it short, 2-3 minutes. Teach people the basics:

- What documents need notarizing
- How mobile notaries save time
- What to do if you lose your ID before closing

People Google this stuff every day. Show up on YouTube like the pro you are.

Video Ideas:

- What Is a Notary and Why Should You Care?
- 5 Weird Things I've Had to Notarize
- Mobile Notary Myths Busted
- Funniest place I performed as a notary

Don't worry about perfect lighting. Just be real, relatable, and helpful. You'll build trust faster than a phone call from a lawyer's office.

1. **Instagram and TikTok:**

2. Post behind-the-scenes content. Funny client moments. Short educational tips. Show your car setup. Your daily routes. Your favorite pen.

Let people see the *human* behind the notary. Most importantly, let them see that you're *good vibes plus professional service.*

Step Three: Own Your Niche

Notaries can do more than real estate closings and power of attorney documents, which you have read in this great book. Start thinking like a **notarypreneur**.

Want to stand out? Pick a specialty or two. Market them like crazy.

- **Weddings:** Yep. Makes for great videos. That means tuxes, beach ceremonies, and love stories. Not a bad gig.

- **Hospital Notarizations:** Partner with hospital social workers. Families in crisis need fast, legal help. You could be their superhero in scrubs.

- **Jails & Detention Centers:** Tough crowd, but consistent business. Establish yourself as the go-to for legal visits. I can see all kinds of material to post about. You should hear some of my personal jail signing stories.

- **Business Contracts for Startups:** Find local entrepreneurs and offer a Startup Stamp Package, notarize their contracts, NDAs, and investor paperwork.

The more specific you get, the more magnetic you become. **Generalists compete. Specialists dominate.**

Step Four: Be So Professional It's Unexpected

Professionalism is part of the brand, too. But we're not talking boring business cards and stiff handshakes. We're talking modern, smooth, and memorable.

- Branded polo or jacket, easy, clean, and professional
- A slick digital business card (look into Dot or Popl)
- Set appointment confirmations via text or email
- QR code on your car door, clipboard, or bag that links to your reviews
- Google Business Profile: If you don't have one, stop reading and fix that now.

You want people to say, That was easier than I thought... and kinda fun.

Step Five: Collaborate and Cross Promote

Nobody hustles alone. Partner with:

- **Realtors:** offer free workshops on notarization basics for buyers and sellers
- **Loan Officers:** make their job easier, and they'll keep calling
- **Law Firms:** be their emergency backup when their in-house notary's out
- **Senior Centers:** older adults need notarizations all the time. Be their go-to.
- **CCW Certification:** Here, you can double dip. Fingerprinting is necessary for all CCW permits

Offer lunch and learn sessions or create a one-pager showing how you can save them time and hassle. Most people don't even know what a mobile notary is until they desperately need one.

Be ready when the bat signal goes up.

Step Six: Make It Memorable and Shareable

Create little experiences people talk about.

- Leave behind a branded pen. Cheap, but sticky.
- Use a stamp that says "Thank You" on their copy
- Snap a pic with clients (with permission), and share with a quick blurb

You're not just running errands. You're solving legal headaches. That deserves a little celebration.

And if you really want to go next level? Start a segment called "Notary Tales," a blog or video series of wild, heartwarming, or hilarious experiences. Protect identities, of course. But storytelling builds connection. People love a good behind-the-scenes story. Especially when it involves crazy places, surprise weddings, or emotional final wishes.

Bonus Round: Watch and Learn

Here are some YouTube creators doing it right:

- **Notary Stars:** Real-world training and marketing tips
- **Laura Biewer Presents:** Practical advice and niche gold
- **Mark Wills Loan Signing System:** Tons of marketing insight

Take notes, borrow ideas, remix for your own flavor.

Final Word: You're Not Just a Notary

You're a business. A brand. A bridge between people and their next big step. Whether they're buying a house, starting a business, or giving their cousin power of attorney, they need someone sharp, dependable, and human.

This journey started with a notary stamp. It ends with **a business that supports your life, your family, freedom, flexibility, and your future finances.**

You are no longer just a notary.

You are:
The Moment Maker.
The Signature Whisperer.
The Person Who Shows Up

CHAPTER 11

Bonus Bonus Bonus

Key Notes:

The Four F's

Finance, Freedom, Flexibility, Family

I trust these chapters have proven both enlightening and helpful. My sincerest aspiration is that within these pages you have encountered an idea, a perspective, or a strategy capable of meaningfully enriching the trajectory of your life. Share these pages with academic advisors, vocational mentors, and guidance leaders at universities and secondary schools. Allow this work to serve as a lantern for those whose ambitions stretch beyond prescribed vocations. Not all are meant to serve food until their big break or pursue the fleeting applause as an online influencer.

Within the notarial profession lies an expanse of avenues offering control over your schedule, steadiness in income, and the irreplaceable luxury of unbroken hours with those you love. What I have outlined here merely grazes the breadth of potential your commission affords. Engage in rigorous inquiry, examine the niches that speak to your inclinations, and immerse yourself in the arenas that align with your long-term aspirations. For those in California, conducting jail signings, apostilles, and integrating into the bail bond sector stand as highly viable pursuits. The progression toward remote online notarization is the way of the future, and mastering it can change your life.

My contact details rest within these pages, extended as an open invitation for correspondence. Present your inquiries, and I will reply. If an answer eludes me, I will direct you toward one who possesses it. My achievements in both the notarial and bail bond domains were not the result of happenstance; they were cultivated through deliberate study and the honing of expertise. I chose self-determination in work, for I was unsuited to the constraints of traditional employment. I sucked as an employee.

I extend to you my earnest wishes for prosperity and contentment on whichever course you undertake. May your chosen endeavors yield not only material success but also the deeper satisfaction of purpose fulfilled.

Bonus Number One: Wedding Officiant.

Becoming a Wedding Officiant as a Notary
Great Company: Rainbow Wedding Chapel
Selecia Young-Jones
www.904rainbow.com

Step 1: Verify Your State's Authority

State-specific rules: Notaries can perform marriages in states like Florida, South Carolina, and Maine. If you're in one of these states, you can officiate weddings as part of your notary duties without additional licensing.

Check Local Regulations: Always verify with your state's notary division or equivalent agency to ensure you understand any specific regulations or additional requirements.

Step 2: Obtain Necessary Credentials

Ordination: If your state requires additional credentials beyond your notary status, you may need to become ordained. This process can often be completed online through organizations like the Universal Life Church or American Marriage Ministries. Ordination typically costs between $20 to $50.

Notary Commission: Ensure your notary commission is current and in good standing. This is essential for performing any duties legally recognized under your notary authority.

Step 3: Understand the Legal Requirements

Marriage License Compliance: Familiarize yourself with the requirements for signing marriage licenses in your state, including any waiting periods or documentation you must verify before officiating a ceremony.

Record Keeping: Learn the process for submitting completed marriage licenses to the appropriate government office, ensuring that the marriage is legally recognized.

Step 4: Develop Your Services

Ceremony Planning: Offer a range of ceremony options, from religious, traditional, and contemporary to personalized scripts, to accommodate different couples' preferences. Consider developing packages that might include rehearsal attendance and custom vows.

Religious Ceremony Script Sample:

[Opening Remarks]

Officiant: Dearly beloved, we are gathered here today in the sight of God and these witnesses to join [Partner 1] and [Partner 2] in holy matrimony. As we celebrate this sacred union, let us remember that love is patient, love is kind, and it does not envy or boast.

[Vows]

Officiant: [Partner 1], do you take [Partner 2] to be your lawfully wedded spouse, to live together in the holy covenant of marriage? Will you love, honor, and cherish [Partner 2], in sickness and in health, as long as you both shall live?

Partner 1: I do.

Officiant: [Partner 2], do you take [Partner 1] to be your lawfully wedded spouse, to live together in the holy covenant of marriage? Will you love, honor, and cherish [Partner 1], in sickness and in health, as long as you both shall live?Partner 2: I do.

[Rings]

Officiant: May these rings be a symbol of your vows and a reminder of the love you share. [Partner 1], please place the ring on [Partner 2]'s finger and repeat after me: With this ring, I thee wed.

[Pronouncement]

Officiant: By the power vested in me by the state and the divine, I now pronounce you husband and wife. You may kiss your bride!

Traditional Ceremony Script Sample:

[Opening Remarks]

Officiant: Ladies and gentlemen, we are gathered here today to witness and celebrate the union of [Partner 1] and [Partner 2]. Marriage is a promise, a potential made in the heart of two people who love each other and takes a lifetime to fulfill.

[Vows]

Officiant: [Partner 1], do you take [Partner 2] as your lawfully wedded spouse, to have and to hold from this day forward, for better, for worse, for richer, for poorer, in sickness and in health, to love and to cherish, until death do you part?

Partner 1: I do.

Officiant: [Partner 2], do you take [Partner 1] as your lawfully wedded spouse, to have and to hold from this day forward, for better, for worse, for richer, for poorer, in sickness and in health, to love and to cherish, until death do you part?

Partner 2: I do.

[Rings]

Officiant: These rings symbolize a never ending circle of love. [Partner 1], place the ring on [Partner 2]'s finger and repeat: With this ring, I thee wed.

[Pronouncement]

Officiant: By the authority vested in me, I now pronounce you husband and wife. You may kiss each other!

Contemporary Ceremony Script Sample:

[Opening Remarks]

Officiant: Welcome, everyone, to the celebration of [Partner 1] and [Partner 2]'s love story. Today, we don't just witness a marriage; we celebrate friendship, laughter, and the odd quirks that make these two perfect for each other.

[Vows]

Officiant: [Partner 1], do you promise to keep [Partner 2] laughing even when they don't find your jokes funny, to support their dreams, and to be their partner in all life's adventures?

Partner 1: I do.

Officiant: [Partner 2], do you promise to love [Partner 1] even when they're hangry, to make spontaneous dance parties a regular thing, and to be their teammate on this crazy ride called life?

Partner 2: I do.

[Rings]

Officiant: May these rings remind you of the beauty in your partnership. [Partner 1], place the ring on [Partner 2]'s finger and say, With this ring, I give you my heart.

[Pronouncement]

Officiant: By the power vested in me, and with great joy, I now pronounce you married. You may kiss!

Non-Religious Ceremony Script Sample:

[Opening Remarks]

Officiant: Friends and family, we are here to witness the union of [Partner 1] and [Partner 2], who stand before us today to declare their love and commitment in a partnership of equals. [Vows] **Officiant**: [Partner 1], do you promise to respect [Partner 2]'s individuality, to stand by them in life's joyful moments and its challenges, and to grow together as equals?

Partner 1: I do.

Officiant: [Partner 2], do you promise to respect [Partner 1]'s individuality, to stand by them in life's joyful moments and its challenges, and to grow together as equals?

Partner 2: I do.

[Rings]

Officiant: These rings symbolize unity and commitment. [Partner 1], place the ring on [Partner 2]'s finger and repeat: I give you this ring as a symbol of my love.

[Pronouncement]

Officiant: By the commitment you have made to each other, I now pronounce you married. You may seal your promise with a kiss!

Step 5: Build Your Network

Collaborate with Wedding Professionals: Connect with local wedding planners, venues, photographers, and florists to expand your network and gain referrals.

Attend Bridal Shows: Participate in bridal expos and shows to meet potential clients and showcase your services.

Marketing Materials: Create promotional materials, including a website, business cards, and social media profiles, to advertise your services.

Step 6: Financial and Administrative Considerations

Pricing Strategy: Research local market rates for officiants to set competitive pricing. Consider offering discounts for repeat clients or referrals.

Liability Insurance: Consider obtaining professional liability insurance to protect yourself against any potential legal claims.

Step 7: Continuous Education and Improvement

Enhance Your Skills: Consider taking public speaking or officiant training courses to improve your presentation and ceremony delivery.

Seek Feedback: After each ceremony, ask for feedback from the couple to refine your services and enhance client satisfaction.

Potential Costs1.

1. Ordination Fee: Generally between $20 and $50, if required.

2. Marketing Expenses: Includes costs for business cards, website development, and advertising, which can range from $100 to $500.

3. Insurance: Liability insurance might cost $200 to $500 annually.

Where to Start Contact Local Authorities: Begin by contacting your state's notary division or equivalent office to clarify your ability to perform marriages and any specific steps required. NNA is always the best place to start your research.Online Resources: Utilize online platforms like the Universal Life Church or American Marriage Ministries to obtain ordination if needed.

By following these steps, you can effectively position yourself as a wedding officiant, offering a valuable service that complements your notary business. If you need specific information for your state or additional guidance, feel free to reach out, and we can research your state together.

Bonus #2: Bail Bond Forms and Script:

If you plan to collaborate with bail bond companies, it's essential to familiarize yourself with key forms specific to the industry. Ensure you consult with the surety company in your state to obtain the correct documents. Keep in mind that each bail bond company operates independently, so don't expect consistency when seeking business opportunities across different firms.

Introduction In-Person Script:

Receptionist: "Hello, how can I help you today?"

You: "Good [morning/afternoon], my name is [Your Name], I wanted to stop by to introduce myself and see if there's someone available whom I can talk to about providing notary services for your company. I'm working with bail bond companies here in Los Angeles. I specialized in collateral signings and Deed of Trust. If you're not 100% hooked on a notary, I would love to be your [Guy/Lady]; if you are, I'd love to be your backup notary. Is it ok if I leave my contact information with you? Thanks"

Deed of Trust:

RECORDING REQUESTED BY

AND WHEN RECORD MAIL TO

——————————————————————— SPACE ABOVE THIS LINE FOR RECORDER'S USE ———————————————

DEED OF TRUST

This Deed of Trust made this _____ day of _____, 20 _____

Between _____, herein called TRUSTOR, and Bankers Surety Services, Inc., herein called TRUSTEE,

and Bankers Insurance Company, herein called BENEFICIARY, WITNESSETH: That Trustor hereby GRANTS to TRUSTEE, IN TRUST, WITH POWER

OF SALE, all that property in the County of _____, in the State of _____, described as:

Lot_____ _____ Block _____ Tract _____ APN _____

as per map recorded in Book, _____ Page _____ or Maps, Official Records

in the office of the County Recorder of _____ County.

Commonly know as _____

    THIS DEED IS FOR THE PURPOSE OF SECURING payment to the said Beneficiary of all monies due to it and of all losses, damages, attorney's fees, private investigation fees, court assessment, bail premium, expenditures and liability suffered, sustained, made or incurred by it (and as more fully set forth in that certain bail bond and/or indemnity agreement(s), which agreement(s) is made a part hereof by reference as though herein fully set forth), on account of, growing out of, or resulting from the execution of a bond or bond(s) on behalf of _____

Bond No._____ in the amount of $ _____ in the matter of _____

_____ vs. _____ ; and/or on

account of, growing out of, or resulting from the execution of any other bail bond executed by the Beneficiary in connection with or relative to the above referred bail bond and/or indemnity agreement(s) and for which amounts, and the matters set forth in the said bail bond and/or indemnity agreement, the property hereinabove referred to, stands as security.

    IT IS AGREED AND CONDITIONED that a certificate signed by the Beneficiary at any time hereafter setting forth that the said bond has been declared forfeited or that a loss, damage, expenditures or liability has been sustained by the Surety or Beneficiary an account of the aforesaid Undertaking: the date or dates and amount or amounts of such loss, damages, attorney's fees, private investigation fees, court assessment, bail premiums, expenditures and/or liability; that payment has been demanded of the party or parties on whose behalf the aforesaid Undertaking was or is about to be executed; and that such loss, damages, expenditures or determined liability has not been paid to the Beneficiary, shall be conclusive and binding on the Trustor, and shall be the warrant of the Trustee to proceed forthwith to foreclose and sell upon the security herein, and from the proceeds of sale (after deduction expenses including cost and search of evidence of title) pay to the Beneficiary the amount so certified, including interest of ten percent per annum from demand to date of payment and attorneys fees.

    IT IS FURTHER AGREED THAT: upon delivery of said Certificate to Trustee, Beneficiary may declare all sums or obligations secured hereby due and payable by delivery to Trustee of written declaration of default and demand for sale and of written notice of default and of election to cause to be sold said property , which notice Trustee shall cause to be duly filed for record.

    IT SHALL BE DEEMED SUFFICIENT if proceedings to foreclose and sell the security herein are executed by any one of the above named Trustees and it shall be deemed sufficient if a full reconveyance is executed by any one of the above named Trustees; and said one Trustee shall be deemed to be the attorney-in-fact for the other Trustees for those purposes. The authority thus granted herein shall be deemed to be coupled with an interest and shall not be affected by the death or incompetency of any of the Trustees for whom such one Trustee shall be acting.

    THE UNDERSIGNED TRUSTOR REQUESTS that a copy of any notice of default and of any notice of sale hereunder be mailed to him at his mailing address opposite his signature hereto. Failure to insert such address shall be deemed a waiver of any request hereunder for a copy of such notices.

SIGNATURE OF TRUSTOR	STREET AND NUMBER	CITY	STATE

State of California   County of _____

On_____, 20_____ before me, _____, a Notary Public, personally appeared

_____

who proved to me on the basis of satisfactory evidence to be the person(s) whose name(s) is/are subscribed to the within instrument and acknowledged to me that he/she/they executed this same in his/her/their authorized capacity(ies), and that by his/her/their signature(s) on this instrument the person(s), or the entity upon behalf of which the person(s) acted, executed the instrument.

I certify under PENALTY OF PERJURY under the laws of the State of California that the foregoing paragraph is true and correct.

WITNESS in my hand and official seal.   (Seal)

_____

Signature of Notary Public

BIC0420790309

Deed of Trust Rent:

AND WHEN RECORDED MAIL TO:

SPACE ABOVE THIS LINE FOR RECORDER'S USE

DEED OF TRUST AND ABSOLUTE ASSIGNMENT OF RENTS

This Deed of Trust with Assignment of Rents, is made this _____ day of, _____ 20_____ by
_____ ("TRUSTOR")

whose address is_____
                                    (number and street)   (City)   (State)   (Zip)
to __Bankers Surety Services, Inc._____ ("TRUSTEE"), for the benefit of___Bankers Insurance Company__

("BENEFICIARY"), whose address is ___P.O. Box 33015, St Petersburg, FL 33733_____, Trustor
irrevocably grants and conveys to Trustee, in Trust, with power of sale, all Trustor's right, title and interest now owned or later acquired
in the following described property located in the County of_____, State of California:

COMMONLY KNOWN AS _____
   Together with all the tenements, hereditaments and appurtenances now or hereafter thereunto belonging or in any way
appertaining, and the rents, issues and profits thereof are herein referred to as the PROPERTY.

   THIS DEED IS FOR THE PURPOSE OF SECURING payment to the said Beneficiary of all monies due to it and of all losses,
damages, attorney's fees, private investigation fees, court assessment, bail premium, expenditures and liability suffered, sustained,
made or incurred by it (and as more fully set forth in that certain bail bond and/or indemnity agreement(s), which agreement(s) is made
a part hereof by reference as though herein fully set forth), on account of, growing out of, or resulting from the execution of a bond
or bond(s) on behalf of_____ Bond No._____ in
the amount of $_____ in the matter of _____ vs.
_____ ; and/or on account of, growing out of, or resulting from the execution of any other bail
bond executed by the Beneficiary in connection with or relative to the above referred bail bond and/or indemnity agreement(s) and for
which amounts, and the matters set forth in the said bail bond and/or indemnity agreement, the property hereinabove referred to, stands
as security.

   To protect the security on this Deed of Trust, Trustor covenants and agrees:
   1. To keep the property in good condition and repair; to permit no waste thereof; to complete any building, structure or
improvement being built or about to be built thereon; to restore promptly any building, structure or improvement thereon which may be
damaged or destroyed; and to comply with all laws, ordinances, regulations, covenants, conditions and restrictions affecting the
property.
   2. To pay before delinquent all lawful taxes and assessments upon the property; to keep the property free and clear of all other
charges, liens or encumbrances impairing the security of this Deed of Trust.
   3. To keep all buildings now or hereafter erected on the property described herein continuously insured against loss by fire or other
hazards in an amount not less than the total debt secured by this Deed of Trust. All policies shall be held by the Beneficiary, and be in
such companies as the Beneficiary may approve and have loss payable first to the Beneficiary, as its interest may appear, and then to
the Trustor. The amount collected under any insurance policy may be applied upon any indebtedness hereby secured in such order as
the Beneficiary shall determine. Such application by the Beneficiary shall not cause discontinuance of any proceedings to foreclose this
Deed of Trust. In the event of foreclosure, all rights of the Trustor in insurance policies then in force shall pass to the purchaser at the
foreclosure sale.
   4. To defend any action or proceeding purporting to affect the security hereof of the rights or powers of Beneficiary or Trustee, and
to pay all costs and expenses, including cost of title search and attorney's fees in a reasonable amount, in any such action or
proceeding, and in any suit brought by Beneficiary to foreclose this Deed of Trust.
   5. To pay all costs, fees and expenses in connection with this Deed of Trust, including the expenses of the Trustee incurred in
enforcing the obligation secured hereby and Trustee's and attorney's fees actually incurred, as provided by statute.
   6. Should Trustor fail to pay when due any taxes, assessments, insurance premiums, liens, encumbrances or other charges
against the property herein above described, Beneficiary may pay the same, and the amount so paid, with interest at the legal rate, shall
be added to and become a part of the debt secured by this Deed of Trust.

BIC0420290309

Disclosure of Real Property Lien:

CALIFORNIA
DISCLOSURE OF LIEN AGAINST REAL PROPERTY DO NOT SIGN THIS DOCUMENT UNTIL YOU READ AND UNDERSTAND IT!

THIS BAIL BOND WILL BE SECURED BY REAL PROPERTY YOU OWN OR IN WHICH YOU HAVE AN INTEREST. THE FAILURE TO PAY THE BAIL BOND PREMIUMS WHEN DUE OR THE FAILURE OF THE DEFENDANT TO COMPLY WITH THE CONDITIONS OF BAIL COULD RESULT IN THE LOSS OF YOUR PROPERTY!

If the Bond is secured by a real property lien, within 30 days after notice is given by any individual, agency or entity to Surety or its bail producer of the expiration of the time for appeal of the order exonerating the Bond, or within 30 days after the payment in full of all moneys owed on the Bond, whichever is later in time, the Surety or bail producer shall deliver to the person who signed the deed of trust a fully executed and notarized reconveyance of title, a certificate of discharge or a full release of any lien against real property to secure performance of the conditions of the Bond. If a timely notice of appeal of the order exonerating the Bond is filed with the court, that 30-day period shall begin on the date the determination of the appellate court affirming the order exonerating the Bond becomes final. Upon the reconveyance, the Surety or bail producer shall deliver the original note and deed of trust, security agreement or other instrument which secures the Bond obligation to the person who signed that document.

I acknowledge and certify that I have read and understand the above disclosure.

Signed, sealed and delivered this _____ **day of** _____ **, 20____.**

Signature of Property Owner _____

Printed Name of Property Owner _____

Acknowledgement:

CALIFORNIA ALL-PURPOSE
CERTIFICATE OF ACKNOWLEDGMENT

A notary public or other officer completing this certificate verifies only the identity of the individual who signed the document to which this certificate is attached, and not the truthfulness, accuracy, or validity of that document.

State of California

County of _____

On _____ before me, _____,
(Here insert name and title of the officer)

personally appeared _____,

who proved to me on the basis of satisfactory evidence to be the person(s) whose name(s) is/are subscribed to the within instrument and acknowledged to me that he/she/they executed the same in his/her/their authorized capacity(ies), and that by his/her/their signature(s) on the instrument the person(s), or the entity upon behalf of which the person(s) acted, executed the instrument.

I certify under PENALTY OF PERJURY under the laws of the State of California that the foregoing paragraph is true and correct.

WITNESS my hand and official seal.

_____   (Notary Seal)
Signature of Notary Public

ADDITIONAL OPTIONAL INFORMATION

DESCRIPTION OF THE ATTACHED DOCUMENT

_____
(Title or description of attached document)

_____
(Title or description of attached document continued)

Number of Pages _____ Document Date _____

_____
(Additional information)

CAPACITY CLAIMED BY THE SIGNER
☐ Individual (s)
☐ Corporate Officer
_____
(Title)
☐ Partner(s)
☐ Attorney-in-Fact
☐ Trustee(s)
☐ Other _____

INSTRUCTIONS FOR COMPLETING THIS FORM

Any acknowledgment completed in California must contain verbiage exactly as appears above in the notary section or a separate acknowledgment form must be properly completed and attached to that document. The only exception is if a document is to be recorded outside of California. In such instances, any alternative acknowledgment verbiage as may be printed on a document so long as the verbiage does not require the notary to do something that is illegal for a notary in California (i.e. certifying the authorized capacity of the signer). Please check the document carefully for proper notarial wording and attach this form if required.

- State and County information must be the State and County where the document signer(s) personally appeared before the notary public for acknowledgment.
- Date of notarization must be the date that the signer(s) personally appeared which must also be the same date the acknowledgment is completed.
- The notary public must print his or her name as it appears within his or her commission followed by a comma and then your title (notary public).
- Print the name(s) of document signer(s) who personally appear at the time of notarization.
- Indicate the correct singular or plural forms by crossing off incorrect forms (i.e. he/she/they, is /are) or circling the correct forms. Failure to correctly indicate this information may lead to rejection of document recording.
- The notary seal impression must be clear and photographically reproducible. Impression must not cover text or lines. If seal impression smudges, re-seal if a sufficient area permits, otherwise complete a different acknowledgment form.
- Signature of the notary public must match the signature on file with the office of the county clerk.
  ❖ Additional information is not required but could help to ensure this acknowledgment is not misused or attached to a different document.
  ❖ Indicate title or type of attached document, number of pages and date.
  ❖ Indicate the capacity claimed by the signer. If the claimed capacity is a corporate officer, indicate the title (i.e. CEO, CFO, Secretary).
- Securely attach this document to the signed document.

Motivational Quotes

1. "Faith is taking the first step even when you don't see the whole staircase." Martin Luther King Jr.

2. "The only way to discover the limits of the possible is to go beyond them into the impossible." Arthur C. Clarke

3. "Life shrinks or expands in proportion to one's courage." Anaïs Nin

4. "Twenty years from now you will be more disappointed by the things that you didn't do than by the ones you did do." H. Jackson Brown Jr. (often attributed to Mark Twain)

5. "Success is not final, failure is not fatal: It is the courage to continue that counts." Winston Churchill

6. "Do not be too timid and squeamish about your actions. All life is an experiment. The more experiments you make, the better." Ralph Waldo Emerson

7. "You miss 100% of the shots you don't take." Wayne Gretzky

8. "What would life be if we had no courage to attempt anything?" Vincent van Gogh

9. "The future belongs to those who believe in the beauty of their dreams." Eleanor Roosevelt

10. "Man cannot discover new oceans unless he has the courage to lose sight of the shore." André Gide

Now Stop Reading And Go Make It Happen. Let Not Luck Be The Only Reason For Your SUCCESS!

About the Author

Delrae Hemphill is a man of many hats and endless talents! From mobile notary and real estate broker to bail bonds agent and actor, Delrae's resume reads like an action packed movie script. But wait, there is more! He is also a published author, father, and mentor, spreading his wisdom and creativity like confetti wherever he goes. When you chat with Delrae, you will quickly realize he is a whirlwind of energy with a knack for turning complex ideas into accessible nuggets of gold. His latest book, Mobile Notary Side Hustle or Business, is just another testament to his gift for distilling knowledge and giving back to the community. After diving into his insights, do not be surprised if you find yourself adding Delrae to your Christmas card list because this is one gift that keeps on giving. Bravo, Delrae! My friend you have done it again, and we cannot wait to see what you come up with next.

Terry Lewis

www.ingramcontent.com/pod-product-compliance
Lightning Source LLC
Chambersburg PA
CBHW051225120626
46547CB00013B/1506